Sticked

Stoned

&

Bottled

Scott Gibson

With grateful thanks to my friends and readers Michaela Kahn, Christien Gohlson, and Erin Dobyns, my father and stepmother Ray and Kathy Gibson, and my son Thomas Gibson (for his patience during the completion of this book).

On the day of this typing, this day in history, February 8, 2014, the United States Attorney General Eric Holder announced sweeping changes in the Justice Department's handling of same sex married couples, including granting all of the same legal federal rights as opposite sex couples.

Edited by Scott Gibson
Blood & Tears, Poems for Matthew Shepard
Painted Leaf Press, NYC 1999.

SCOTT GIBSON

Sticked
Stoned
&
Bottled

a poem
a discussion

New Shrine
Boulder Colorado

Sticked Stoned & Bottled.
Copyright © 2014 by Scott Gibson.

All rights reserved. No part of this book may be used or reproduced in any manner whatsoever without written permission from the publisher except in the case of brief quotations embodied in critical articles and reviews.

New Shrine
A division of Omnia Om Ltd.

For permissions, contact the Publisher:
omniaom.com/contact

Cover design by Scott Gibson.

ISBN: 978-1-942378-00-6

For guys and girls living this life—

Don't fret. Some will only understand upon croaking.

They just better not get in our way...

TABLE OF CONTENT

white	9
broken	11
human	19
magic	23
tear	27
shatter	31
bone	33
sandpaper	37
shard	41
outburst	45
cloud	47
spread/veil	51
mold	55
shark	57
rain	59
chain	63
wave	65
plastic	69
glass	73
saint	75
armor	79
gate	83
impulse	87
ground	91
spice	95
uncle	97
shore	101
cement	105
snow	107
solo	109

the beginning

It is a wandering mind that
seeks to rest somewhere—
words will never hurt you
these words, not of sight nor color
nor of what they demand—
I have only found interest
in their meanings and sounds and
I like them. Or perhaps

they remind me of sharded glass—
weapons
I've grown to know through magnified
wounds, these gashes—

it is *not true*, that rhyme
            those words

WHITE

(adj.) the color of pure snow, the margins of this page, etc. reflecting nearly all waves of sunlight (human beings); marked by slight pigmentation of skin whose racial heritage is Caucasian, *a white club, a white neighborhood*; pallid or pale as from fear or other strong emotion, *white with rage*; lacking color, transparent (white fags); *Politically.* ultraconservative, morally pure, innocent; to be or cause to be deprived of one's resources, *dishonesty is bleeding the church white*; (n.) in the white, in an unfinished state or condition; (often cap.) a member of a royalist, conservative, or reactionary political party; to censor as by obliterating words or passages with white; without malice, harmless but hoarse, providing confusion like thunder (white thunder) rain on the edges; *Entomol.* any of several white-winged butterflies of the family Pieridae.

Love your enemies! Pray for those who persecute you! In that way, you will be acting as true children of your Father in heaven.[1]

there it was
fresh ice
on a branch, white
crystal edges
on the outside
empty like
jumbled sands around it
(this bottle)
the sun-burnt tree
was a tree,
black crusted, opaque
and tiny like glass
shards, my heart was
(stuffed in, un-plunged)

When lawlessness is abroad in the land, the same thing will happen here that happened in Nazi Germany. Many of those people involved in Adolf Hitler were Satanists, many of them were homosexuals, the two things seem to go together; it is a pathology, it is a sickness.[2]

BROKEN

(adj.) reduced to parts, ruptured, torn, fractured like the metal pick, carefully corrupted, not functioning properly like earth, thorn in skin, handle with care, caress with passion, with ice. *Of sky cover.* more than half, but not half, covered with blankets, with white, with clouds, comma, (also scattered); changing direction abruptly as a mirror (ufo), a facsimile printed on a broken line made of mud, petrified like taffy, unchanged or incomplete, another infringement or violation, *the broken glass forms from sand*, from sleep, from tears, another glass, another violation, interrupted, returning to broken sleep, (be sad with me—do not wipe those eyes) disrupted, weakened in strength, encrusted, (spirit) reduced to submission, I have removed you from myself, (imperfectly) spoken like language, are you mad? Are you normal? Under emotional strain, disunited, divided, an open door, no, cracked open like a hot trunk, cracked

cute white cornered on the east side,
(rough, irregular) ruined.

♣♣♣♣♣

> When I was in the military, they gave me a medal for killing
> two men and a discharge for loving one.[3]

        the leafless
stems of that torso,
stubborn, still
bold, but without
determined placement,
without its sweet guts,
no red juice
or sap, yet somehow
beans, somewhat
white as bleach,
oddly fired
marshmallow white
dried tears
on my cheek,
they stood like beasts,
broad, elegant
    I went to the gym
    for months, for
    muscles, a look
    of luxury, for forearms
and pits like temples

> *Involvement in homosexuality can kill you. It can kill you
> emotionally, it can kill you physically, and it can certainly kill
> you spiritually.*[4]

                        they're
laughing at me,
my stories, my
two dimensional
spheres, they're playing
resuscitation games
on this stomach with
stones and sticks, they're
singing, light gray,
white, and clouded
diamond raindrops
named John (a raindrop)
in white, full
of heat and salt,
quoting pope,
though still empty, all
hopeless inside
the bottle,
the clear glass,
filmed
with smoke,
burning butts,
fags again, inside
the bottle
extinguished
        though in the white
        cloudless sky
        a flute, an open door
        and cool breezes
we bask
in the sun, desperately

avoiding the fire, carelessly
shirking the ash

> *Homosexuals are included in a list of sinners, who, if unrepentant, will not inherit the kingdom of God.*[5]

[white
really exists and
black smells
damp, tastes like
feathers and veils,
and the walls around it
are navy, distant, a pink
bubble-gum lolli, pantless
and covered with ants,
this sucker is,
an intense light
image of bolts,
of rubber, of
death, *the tongue,*
blue rubber lips
   closed around it]

> *The sexual revolution, of which homosexual activism is a key part, has laid waste to countless lives, destroyed families, and shattered hopes for people who have been cast adrift into a deadly carnival of excess. It's time to reaffirm the permanent things of marriage and family and sexual sanity. It's time to throw people a life preserver instead of a life destroyer, which the homosexual subculture surely is.*[6]

                    [I
was able to smell him
once, burrito, tortilla]

                    I want
to see him housed
in ditches of snow,
          [white does exist]
perhaps we should drink
our wine, lick it
off the moon, off Africa
or Mexico, the soft pink
dripping pink, that
of thunder, painted
on the inner walls
of my ribcage,
I am an artist,
          no, I was
          until sixth grade, until
          the stick
          was inserted
into my—and
my eyes,
my flamboyant
eyes, my girly eyes,
glossed over,
          bottled

> *Satan uses homosexuals as pawns. They're in, as you know, key positions in media, they're in the White House, they're in everything, they're in Hollywood now. Then, unfortunately, after he uses them, he infects them with AIDS and then they die.*[7]

                        this
was the sky, transparent—
it sang pop bottles
and sweet bubbles
until they cracked
open, breath
like gamma and
peppermint, together with
hot water balancing
on a sternum [there is
no "I" without it]
without the sliced rays
of mangos or love letters
spilled fuchsia plum
without tie-up
ties, no mess
in the clip-on,
        [mom wouldn't have it
        in the pews]
not made for ease but
with ease, with
a strong, flat iron hand,
not a simple vein
or a drip from
silver droplets,
        I hide now, speak
        in metaphors
        obviously—
not sweat in textiles that
suffocate humans,
none of this, she thought,

though she only said,
    "it just doesn't look nice."

Imagine a call for 'Sodomite's rights.' In order to get around this distasteful, but accurate image, they have created the terminology 'Gay rights.'[8]

HUMAN

(adj.) having the nature of people, cold, callused, petrified, unable to express kindness, may refer to good and bad characteristics alike, contrasted to divine, to err is human, to fuck is divine, I am only human, pronounced yooman, the social aspects, the characters, want (I want) to be nice, to open a hand, to charge for a smile, to kill (can you see through the glass? the bottle? the broken bottle consists of ego) this is wrong, this capital D, this characteristic called humane, called (sympathetic?) a stick vibrating on skin, red skin, no white, of shattered bottles, I can see through all of it, you claim to be a professor, and still I teach you.

If the Supreme Court says that you have the right to consensual [gay] sex within your home, then you have the right to bigamy, you have the right to polygamy, you have the right to incest, you have the right to adultery.[9]

                        the house
of a larger size
is beside me, quiet
            [and we must be
            quiet]. The tree
is beautiful, dead tree yet
revitalized, hands
on its stomach, it tastes
our energy, *it could be love*
even the stones
have life, all wet,
they rested with warmth until
the tides swung, until
the moon shifted
slightly westward
and the clouds rolled
to the cliffs, it wondered
for a moment about
those hands [the bottle]
hands with cold
calluses and bruised
muscles, the median
of roads, of boulevards,
            though trusted voices profess
            mindless fuckery
untamed, groomed
without mind
of the purple autumn
            [within which, I hid
            and sometimes still]
or mountains eastward,
there too, their magic,
turning seeds

to corn with the sound
of a leaf
    stepped upon

For nearly 4,000 years, since the ancient inhabitants of Sodom fueled the fires of God's wrath, sodomites have been called faggots, contracted to fags. It is an elegant metaphor. Faggots in nature are sticks of wood that burn quick, hot and long, and are hence used to fuel the fires of nature. Etymology, history, and Scripture all endorse and sanctify the usage of faggot or fag to refer to sodomites because sodomites ignite the fires of divine wrath, promised by God himself to destroy any society that elevates homosexuality to a position of wide acceptance and respect.[10]

MAGIC

(n.) the art of producing illusions, sleight of hand, the cold hand, deceptive, art of incantation, of chanting, of calling up goddesses; a technique assuring control of the supernatural (will someone please help me?) *magic shocked the illness from my body* (I am a wizard of great magic) I am mystical influence, the magic of music, the genius of dance, the therapist, encrypted messages, *Japanese*, the enchantment of Asia, of islands, of cultures (of smoothness, not in voice like evening mothers, but in fine lines below belly buttons, in chests) necromancy, sorcery, witchcraft, look at the wall, it's blue and black and stained with blood; what kind of magician are you? am I?

♣♣♣♣♣♣

America is not big enough to shake her fists in the face of a holy God and get away with it... As America has permitted homosexuality to establish itself as an alternate lifestyle, it is also reeling from the frightening spread of sexually transmitted diseases. Sin begets its own consequence, both on individuals and nations.[11]

           slipped apart
like classical musicians,
the fawn
viola once played
of the bottle—
it crashed and
exploded for a moment
like cinnamon, like sand,
like angry sand—
      she dies too,
      and he, the unsexed
      at ten years
      and her, Christian mom
how dare you
my family, bruised, stoned

For everyone who exalts himself will be humbled, and he who humbles himself will be exalted.[12]

          [he said
the tree
was beautiful
and something about
jumbo chalk,
then placed a quarter
inside his painting
on the earth, heads
down, it's worth
more than the penny
pulled from his pocket,

his left hand drew
dice on the hard mud,
he laughed softly
and celebrated
those hands]
        humbled
    by the bills of
    elephants, though
    they are not
    themselves, You
are three people, three
separate people, not pieces,
parts or personalities,
You are three
whole beings, You
have a green ego, a gray
ego, and yet a separate
pink ego, Your hairs
are even different
and Your eyes,
full, soft
burgundy fire
O the tear
on Your cheek, how I could
be that tear

   The biggest hypocrite in the world is the person who believes in the death penalty for murderers but not for homosexuals.[13]

    that tear
is now my son's, we
were three, the same family

the same home,
humble, guarded by
a wooden fence, stakes
sturdy in earth,
then the thunder

TEAR

(n.) drop of saline, watery fluid,
moisten to clear foreign particles, to
clear emotion (esp. grief) something
resembling this, molded to seem as
this, magical, look at me in the eyes,
my tears taste like sperm, like armpits
and worked lips, serving to lubricate
the eyes. Can you see yet? No, I mean
see. Glassmaking. decorative air bubble
enclosed in a glass vessel, a bottle
(esp. grief) of the vessel, the box, the
closed casket, candlelight between,
upon rooftops, sat upon, upon black
shingles, looks like death, smells like

> Someone must not be afraid to say 'moral perversion is wrong.'
> If we do not act now, homosexuals will 'own' America. If you
> and I do not speak up now, the homosexual steamroller will
> literally crush all decent men, women, and children who get in
> its way... and our nation will pay a terrible price.[14]

Your
"maybe," Your
"sort of," the ones
You don't know

are cacti
on dry rural plains,
fields stinging of
bumble bees, roaring
lightning, and
it surrounds You,
surrounds
me like a bookmark.
        [they
say heaven is
bright light,
and white like coconut
bleached socks,
baby teeth white,
white as ocean
and sand dunes,
that hell is dark,
cavernous, dungeon-
like, no escape, though
dark has meant
cold to me.
I sweat in sunlight.
    What is this
    darkness, this
    coldness
    I crave in this
    sunlight?

      We Stand with Chick-fil-A: Marriage Is One Man, One Woman.[15]

    it wasn't
difficult to shatter

the white or the clearest
structure, that bench
upon which the gavel
rested and breathed
hatred, the bench
of a million fish
to stare upon, to
ponder,
to produce illumination,
gallop as a rose does
on a metal drum, to rest
clear stones in sand,
pocket lint in
fingernails, or cake
on newlywed
face, a face
in the bottle, again
the bottle, *discarded*
behind clear
      white
ashen fog, smoke
a fag, slide the butt
into the bottle,
      discard

Legally destroying the exclusive territory of marriage to achieve a political end will not provide the real benefits of marriage to homosexuals, but it may be the blow that the shattered American family does not survive.[16]

SHATTER

(v.) to break (something) into pieces, as by a blow, a knockout, *the shattering of dreams*, of destinies, or perhaps of clear glass bottles (just perhaps, now) to damage by breaking or crushing, *my ship was shattered by the storm*, by acts of violence, human (to 1700, sp. humane) perhaps natural, to weaken, to destroy, refute ideas, opinions, memories, cold memories broken into fragments, *a constant shattering*; German, schmetterling, a butterfly become weak or insubstantial (is this how you look at me?)

Those who practice homosexuality embrace a culture of death. They risk their lives as well as their spiritual well-being…a band of radical activists, many of them highly placed, put the well being of all society at risk to satisfy their craving for approval.[17]

don't forget
to unplug the top
with white thumb or

red knuckle,
> [such events
> are those
> of chosen
> roads, metal
> coffee mug
> turned to
> bone, turned
> to casket]
decayed a hundred
years, inside the cavity—
the cause of it,
the rotting bone

> *Do to others whatever you would like them to do to you. This is the essence of all that is taught in the law and the prophets.*[18]

> and such
> is grace
> such is
this rotting house
> *this bone*
this powdered sugar
bleached, chin with broken
hip and still
this mindless fuckery

> *This is a very serious matter, because it is our children who are the prize for this community; they are specifically targeting our children.*[19]

BONE

(n.) *anat.* one of many structures composing the skeleton, the possible skinless sorcerer, the composite canon, the vertebrae, or the hard connective tissue, my shoes around the ankles, retreat (from the skeleton, skinless) composed of a collagen-rich organic matrix, the dimensions unknown like that of religion, of God, impregnated with calcium and phosphate, (next is to be praised) such a structure from an edible animal, usually with meat adhering to it, clinging, decayed on its edges as an article of food, *pea soup should be made with a hambone,* or a human finger, again humane, (corrupted) ivory whalebone; a concession meant to pacify, *the administration threw the protesters a bone,* forty days in jail, help me retreat, skinless, boneless, (let his bones rest in peace), let my bones decay in peace, *pan down;* to think or feel intuitively, without thinking, the minimum, *I am chilled to the bone,* to have no fear or objection to, to disagree, to argue, to call me

names, to tell me again that I am sick,
to remove the guts, decay the bones

♣♣♣♣♣

> *There are people who were gay and lived the gay lifestyle and aren't anymore. I don't know if that's the similar situation or that's the case for anyone that's black. It's a behavioral issue as opposed to a color of the skin issue, and that's the difference for serving in the military.*[20]

        sharp honey
drips crescent moons
in waves,
sweat from cliffs
of moons, which do I
choose, whom do I
fuck, not him, not
her, no, not her,
him with hiked
legs, chiseled
teeth, fingertip painting
my skin, and coconut
smile, it's too much,
too bold to trap, too
shallow without
a needle in the foot,
men in penguin garb
gawking, curled eyebrows,
pages of swords
folded underneath,
hidden in my erection
it was there, against

Colorado stone
against clergy
against the shards in eyes
the message inside
them, against every color,
every shade
of blue, it wasn't blue,
it was white—
clear, notice it *was*
now disappeared
like midnight, like
the train,
too fast like vodka
on the tongue,
gland and siren
sandpaper yellow
on slanted walls, silence
in a white barn like
drunk butterflies, whacked—
a breeze through
this brush,
a light breeze
     and sudden

> Basically homosexuality is a neurosis. It's healable, it's treatable. We are ministering to 6000 former homosexuals in the Exodus network. Basically, homosexuality is a stunting of psychosexual growth. They are children inside, and any parent out there, you know. When your kid is spoiled, he'll keep coming at you and coming at you until you give him a whack on the bottom and say, "Enough." And then the child will stop.[21]

SANDPAPER

(n.) generally used for smoothing or polishing, though not really, but by halting any metamorphosis with a few words, another handful of pacifiers, or another bone, *the administration threw the protesters sandpaper;* strong fingers coated with a layer of dust, paper thin, but abrasive like sand; any of the rough skin on fingers of reverends or doctors with radio or tv shows or websites that sift the wings of butterflies without remorse, a halting of passions; to shake a finger at, like a vibrator over the nose, to quit emoting, to cause a neighbor pain by careful meditation on guts of formerly beautiful things like gray cotton, to remove the dreams of children, to brainwash, insert sandpaper under blind child's hands, to scrub the minds of those with society, day one, sight will kill, plug your ears, do not think, sandpaper to skull

> *Homosexual activists have made such strides as gaining acceptance that now they feel the final frontier is the children.*[22]

              fingertips
on the back of
my neck,
the hairline; paint
thinner runs
on masterpieces, graffiti
muralled like tears and
cotton candy. Battlefields,
intertwined shoelaces, or
races, the hope
of a balanced knot
      [I am the sweat
      on the back
      of your neck]
questions form
in the heads of steel,
stone-like heads,
quarter sized
and drifting, I choose
the bag of blue
soil, the saints of choice, the
unchoosable, do I really
choose? do I point
a finger? do I
throw stones?

> *I would suggest to you that while the homosexual population may right now be one to two percent, hold your breath people, because the recruitment is loud, it is clear, it is everywhere.*

You'll be seeing, I would say, twenty percent or more, probably thirty percent, or even more than that, of the young population will be moving into homosexual activity.[23]

        here
I sing in fields
of birthday cakes and
subtle silence, hidden bottles
of pheromones
under sifted covers,
sheet and satin, silk
and solid stone,
quarter shy and now
the belly grows with it
expands in possibility
in placid lakes
upstream, in gardens—
        I'm the carrot buried
        in mud, in ash, I'm
        the orange tip with eyes
        pointed downward,
            [I'm stuck
            in a pregnant
            society of norms]
tones in fingertips, constant
a rainbow of waves
turning gray,
an eagle's gray
and where have I gone to,
why haven't I held
the clear bottle, crushed it
with sandpaper—

    quarter grit.
Why haven't my hands
been cupped
around stones,
why haven't they held
the lightning shards,
sticks washed
to extended blankets
on beaches,
picnic baskets and lunch?
Is it because my hands
are still glued
inside my pockets?
        my eyes in mirrors?

Militant homosexuality is fundamentally opposed to religion, family, and anything that presupposes a natural moral order, a transcendent God, or something else higher than ourselves. The activist homosexual agenda and worldview are fundamentally incompatible with Christianity or any form of true religion, because homosexuality is ultimately narcissism.[24]

SHARD

(n.) a fragment of God, esp. of broken
earthenware, shattered earth, brushed
away but not resurrected, broken
human; *Zoology*, a scale with which to
weigh possibilities or broken bones,
pre-human, a shell, as of an egg or a
snail, a hiding place, secret, a closet,
may I return there, please— I wish
not to become another fragment—
shard, (to 1000 AD) sceard, schaard;
akin to shear; (v.) to cut, to slice, by
means of a sharp tool, all those
words, all the sticks and stones, all
this traffic, these tossable, launchable
bottles and stones, the shards of glass;
a Matthew; a Shepard

*You know, really, when you think about it, let me just be blunt
here, when an individual "comes out" and proclaims their
homosexuality, really, what they are doing is standing up and
saying, "I'm a sexual deviant, and I'm proud of it."*[25]

        perhaps
the nudity
underneath the "I"

has gone further
underneath, under
the clear names
of mountain peaks,
under the stone, pockets
of flesh pasted and trapped
in stones, of snow
captured like crimson
in rain, the talent inside
stretched sideways
to the floor then
heel to sky, cobbled
rain in mountain steam,
heal to toe like
letters, handwritten
art, canvas layered
gently, piano
in background, quarter notes
and shyness—
O may I become
               that painting

> *I think that actually AIDS is a guardian. That is I think it was sent, if you would, about forty years ago, to destroy western civilization unless we change our sexual ways. So it's really a Godsend.*[26]

           horses
stolen like
little things, a leaf,
blade of grass
again a caterpillar
a baby's first taste

of juice, of flight
> *freedom*
that phrase spoken
under breath, under
no control, inside the unchosen
and I am sickened,
the sandpaper skin
rubbed together

> *Unless we get medically lucky, in three or four years, one of the options discussed will be the extermination of homosexuals.*[17]

        rules
of the first touch
seem saddened, often
by re-visions of outbursts
unbearable
though real enough
to be discussed,
    actually pondered
and how may it happen—
gas showers, steam-rolled,
lined up and
shot, or AIDS—wrath of—

OUTBURST

(n.) a sudden and violent release, a blow, an outpouring of fists, jabs with elbows, an outburst of tears, an outburst of chalked voice written in white, scribed on the inside, on the skin, on every fucking memory, *can you hear your outburst echo in the strata?* a sudden spell of activity, energy, patterns on sand, on soul, a public disturbance, a riot, esp. in America, an outburst of angry fags, on the blink, flutter of eyelids, batter of man, a service call unanswered, a bursting forth, eruption, there is something to look forward to inside bottles, inside the closed door of the closet, *outburst and be free,* hand firmly gripping the bottle

For the sake of our children and society, we must oppose the spread of homosexual activity. Just as we must oppose murder, stealing, and adultery. Since homosexuals cannot reproduce, the only way for them to "breed" is to recruit. And who are their targets for recruitment? Children.[28]

           there are sounds
of birds
singing, trampling like
cigarette butts, trampling
like dust, a militaristic
force. Tear out
my eyes,
rip off
my ears. Sea, cover me
with your palms
at the ocean floor
with words heard
by empires—
      the warrior and
      the civilian
by other bottles
without the neatly folded
white, without
      perfect clouds

> *The homosexual movement is a progressive outgrowth of the sexual revolution of the past 40 years and will lead to the normalization of even more deviant behavior.*[29]

CLOUD

(n.) visible collection of water or ice suspended in air, usually above the earth's surface, that inevitably forms scars, shards upon the sand, upon the paper cliffs; a dim or obscure area in something usually clear, as if a lie has been told, transparent, *a cloudy spot*, anything that darkens something, religion (doctors of the mind) causes gloom, a cloud in the sky, its shadow casts darkness, absent mindedness, under suspicion; (v.) to overspread, to overshadow, to cloud kindness with religion, to cloud the truth, to be wary of the truth, to be religious, or dishonest; able to be seen without squinting, without thinking, to reveal one's distress, anxiety, *my brow clouded with sadness,* with anger; fog, haze, mist, to haze, to beat up as part of an initiation, connotations of daydreaming, illusions

If we discovered that being a serial killer or a sociopath was genetic, though we might not blame the serial killer or sociopath

for being so, we certainly would not allow him to act up his serial killing or sociopathological disposition.[30]

    inside
I vibrate
heartbeats, images
yellow grasses
on Venus, the drinking
glass unbroken
turns ice (liquid)
inside (reformed)
trapped, my heart
in ribcage, inside
the talent, eloquent
thought—
even limbs hide
sometimes in books
and bed sheets
black light and purple
stomach, see past me, look
through me, erase
the clouds and still
there's no place
for politics in the church
I've heard, and nobody
can make me believe it

Conceiving the militant homosexual movement to pose the greatest threat to the survival of this nation, and that the government in all its branches (including the courts) is caving in to this anti-majoritarian law-trained pervert elite with their specious arguments couched in the inapposite language of civil rights law, and that the churches are likewise crumbling to their

> *junk theology and snake oil pitchman rhetoric which is nothing but heretical sophistry – Westboro Baptist Church has determined to act. The Destroyer of Sodom is not dead. If the same conditions prevail, God's wrath will destroy America just as it did Sodom and Gomorrah in 1898 B.C.*[31]

   the pages
still turn in every notebook
and the sealed ones
speak silently
to their readers, too many
written of
and prayed for
to be silent, to stand
behind corners
packaged up
and placed on the top
shelf, frozen with
sweet vegetables, a loaf
of bread on sale
day old
from the organic grocer
or my own back yard
from the tree
the favorite one that
sheds sticks and whips,
   the willow with arms
   climbable and comforting, eyes
   at water level
   now, waves
   stinging eyes,
orange waves, blue waves
opal waves and rain, the fire

is spending, the fire wants
to spread
into trees that have
veins, even the dead ones
   the ones with veins

> *As with smoking, homosexual behavior's 'second hand' effects threaten public health....Thus, individuals who choose to engage in homosexual behavior threaten not only their own lives, but the lives of the general population.*[32]

SPREAD/VEIL

(v.) to draw or stretch over a flat surface, a veil to hide behind, to stretch out or unfurl into the air as wings or a flag, to distribute over a great distance or period of time, to draw out, a trial, the death of a fag, of a child, cold in the clouded ground, the sandy ground, soil finally enriched with a soul, gentle; to display, on display, gawked at, challenged with infamy, dispose or distribute, apply a thin layer or coating, again a veil; (n.) a piece of opaque or transparent material worn over the face, esp. over the eyes (nor can I see you, or the possibilities) *veiled by suspicion,* usually providing concealment or protection from the elements, the naked hand, a rubber wrist, the fingertips like sandpaper; a part of the headdress of a nun, religion (may I become a woman, still in girl status?) lies, the life of a nun, a mask, disguise or pretense, to find happiness under a veil of hell, the rubber wheels of sports cars, fence after fence, I am happy to be a fag,

can you hear my discomfort, can you
hear my lies, can you see beneath my
veil like you are the corked bottle?

♣♣♣♣♣

*Homosexuality is a decision. It's not a race. People from all
different ethnic backgrounds live in this lifestyle. But people
from all different backgrounds also are liars and cheaters and
malicious and back-stabbing.*[33]

       the painters
continue life's texture
though only wide
enough to make that
perfect line of skin
itch like granite,
the bark
lovely like
stripped wooden fences
and yellow lines
on highways, the "I"
is again gone,
it has chosen to hide
with the bottle,
they were my hands,
my fingers which
parted oceans
of sand, blue crystals,
which spread to allow
the sewable
glass to drop
      rest,

[dolls speak
triangles and lines
combined, sun through
shallow water, Hell red,
take me from this Hell,
ruby red, evil ruby fire,
the footsteps, the rhythm
of footsteps, square
footsteps, aerobic
on wooden porches, a board
cracked through, it
has changed, mars
orbiter, Venus
under earth, a doll
crying stones]
a doll crying.
Uncovered and careful (I
knew nothing of
tides, I knew nothing of
sticky fingers) or mold
in hair, or of colored
rice or cabinets
that needed to be wiped,
I knew nothing of
men in black suits
boys in flannel
sun on their necks

Rights. RIGHTS! RIGHTS? For deviant...sexual behavior there are now rights? That's what I'm worried about with the pedophilia and the bestiality and the sadomasochism and the cross-dressing. Is this all going to be "rights" too, to deviant sexual behavior? It's deviant sexual behavior.[34]

MOLD

(n.) loose, friable earth, esp. rich in organic matter like dead fags and children, favorable to growth in plants; *Brit.* ground, earth, dust, ashes to ashes, goodbye practical earth, a mold of jelly; hollow matrix giving a specific shape, a prototype, example, a distinctive nature, character, *a person of a simple mold,* expendable, one of many able to be killed, chopped up, to be rearranged without loss, without notice, take my blankets too, leave me cold, dripping wet, without fish or bread; (v.) to work into a desired form, to have influence in determining the character of, to mold the character of a child, to preach hate, *to mold the character of a fag,* replaceable growth, a fungus

Homosexuality gave us Adolph Hitler, and homosexuals in the military gave us the Brown Shirts, the Nazi war machine and six million dead Jews.[35]

            I'm afraid
of the taco,
afraid of the artichoke,
and the banana's screams
are green
stakes in the grass
fenced cricket songs
in my rib—
purify my knees, purify
my palms, without
those simple vices
without the scenery
the chocolate
cliffs that lure the blues,
that vacuum the shores
to make them
standable and vast—
            sandless

There are hundreds of children in America who are dying of AIDS because they were sexually abused by homosexuals.[36]

            though beside them, still
are the bamboo seaweeds and
unfertilized eggs of sharks,
    and I live with those
    sharks, and you live
    with those sharks, and
    you live better than me
    because you are not glass,
    you are not bottled,
    you are the stones
    and the sticks

SHARK

(n.) any of a group of elongate
elasmobranch, certain species of
which are large, voracious, and
sometimes dangerous like cock
(though mostly marine fishes) still
nude on the other side of the beach
(origin uncertain) but that don't make
waves or spill blood; a person who
preys greedily on others, usually by
means of cheating or usury or guns
and words; a teacher of this species;
(v.) to obtain by trickery or fraud,
through lies

Many single mothers depend on the association of Boy Scouts for safe, masculine role models to assist them in teaching their sons to be men. A mother's preference for straight men as role models for her children is not bigotry. It is loving concern.[37]

         the sun
is like bath water
unlike a puddle, like
hair on the neck
unlike crisp carrots
and the tree is

beautiful, cotton
eagle, driftwood—
salt drips from my
skin, a cloud
the deep green
thunder and the black
oil rain, without them
I knew of promises, I knew
of islands and sun and
dark legs and capable
possibilities and hands
like machines
and I wanted to be
that statue, but
hunters with sticks
of stone
stood
around campfires
and sang
of rain, they told me
I was only half man,
half human

> To equate homosexuality with race is to give a death sentence to civil rights. No one is enslaving homosexuals… or making them sit in the back of the bus.[38]

RAIN

(n.) water condensed from the
aqueous layer of the skin or the
earth's atmosphere that falls in drops
like sweat (listen as they speak) often
accompanied by thunder (listen)
angry thunder, angry like a mother
whose child was taken, whose fag
child was murdered, a storm, a
shower, *when it rains, it pours;* a heavy
or continuous descent, a rain of
blows; (v.) to fall, to send down in
great quantities, to deal, hurl, fire
repeatedly, to pound continuously, to
murder by hand

> *Not only is homosexuality a sin, but anyone who supports fags*
> *is just as guilty as they are. You are both worthy of death.*[39]

       I beg
the peeled pineapple
crave the garlic
behind his—yes,
how can a crotch
be so nice on such a spider
of a man, his pants a

permeable
holographic loft
a Viper (Utah)
birthday cake on Pier 39
by a pay phone,
their voices inside
my fingernails—
    Adobo, your bright
    fawn color,
    I'm home when I smell it
carpet beige, home
in cathedral iceberg
without windows, without
glass, home
in dark ice, in a clear
plastic trash bag
stretched across my pores
        [did I tell you,
    society is like
    sex, I am gone
    to sex until
    my fingers
    are devoured
    by my teeth or
    wrapped around
    a firm object
    that spews art
    like a pen]

    Gays have sex with "bottles, carrots, even gerbils."[40]

        to function
is to be or just

to smile or just
I guess
to settle with
peanuts and a coke
behind closed doors

Sodomy is a graver sin than murder. – Unless there is life there can be no murder.[41]

[your hair with
bubbles at
the beginning,
somewhere outside
of the blue, searching
elephant tusks
and the grasses
they swept, the poetry
they swept that
resides
in the belly, that
resides in kneecaps, in
nipples touched
lightly with grass-
blades
      in tones
      of tree bark
      painted in rain
      in tones
      of rain, listen]
I heard too, the pleasant
sight of stairwells, upward
into the clouds
to the peaks

they had spoken of
to the stone-slides (though dormant)
to the volcanoes
colorless and cool
and not a movement
was missing, no torpedo
had entered there, and I
begged and begged
for forgiveness, for playful
hands on a cool
summer morning,
refreshed and converted
into chains of
the swing set, upon its
binding leather seat
and something told me
I did not need forgiveness

CHAIN

(n.) a series of objects connected to one another, usually in rings, used for purposes needing flexibility with high strength, used for hauling or mauling; something that binds or restrains (bonds), *chain of timidity,* shackles, a prisoner in chains, bondage and servitude, to live my life in chains, a chain of events, beatings, careful observation of grandparents, careful lies, honest doors for which to hide behind; a distance-measuring device, steel tape, bound; (v.) to confine or restrain, to chain me to a fence and place your hands around my neck, your fists upon my cheek, upon my body, your blood, your chafing voice

What kind of craziness is it in our society which will put a cloak of secrecy around a group of people whose lifestyle is at best abominable. Homosexuality is an abomination. The practices of those people is appalling. It is a pathology. It is a sickness, and instead of thinking of giving these people a preferred status and

*privacy, we should treat AIDS exactly the same way as any
other communicable disease.*[42]

          this was
before the wave, before
the anchor of cast
iron and Teflon
arms—will we continue
to know it, will we
not slip from its surface,
from its open-back skin
like we've forgotten?

*Let your light so shine before men, that they may see your good
works, and glorify your Father which is in heaven.*[43]

we've always forgotten
this surface comes to me
in waves like the bottle, like
the words on its inner
lining, which I can read
and have read
these past twenty years
and was afraid to read
the twenty-one before

*[Homosexuals] want to come into churches and disrupt church
services and throw blood all around and try to give people AIDS
and spit in the face of ministers.*[44]

     please
I see a scarecrow—
its blood

WAVE

(n.) a disturbance on the surface of a liquid body in the form of a moving ridge or swell, a wave of disgust; a widespread feeling, opinion, or tendency, a wave of anti-intellectualism, stupidity, senator, a wave of religious belief, a mass movement of troops, generally used in reference to combat, a fluttering movement made with the hand to signal hello or (usually) goodbye, signaling death, goodbye to Earth, hello to earth (n.) dug up ground, six feet of dirt lifted, tossed aside, and replaced to cover, hide, decay a dead body, human (humane) suffocation, poor children, dirty fags, they belong in the ground, in the dirt; *literary.* a body of water, a sea, ocean, perhaps a puddle, I am small again as an ant, a bug, bothersome, estranged, generally confused, corrupt

If President Obama, Congressional Democrats, and homosexual activists get their wish, your son or daughter may be forced to

> *share military showers and barracks with active and open homosexuals who may very well view them with sexual interest.*[45]

          now
to Mexico, north
to Canada and Alaska,
it knows no geography,
only weather and movement
and landforms
like five hundred yards
six hundred years, prior
in the land unformed
by the white, the
cold white, callused
white, almost, not white
like scuffed outer edges,
broken porcelain
unused or
understood, from which
the sins of heaven
have allowed, were those
the sins of heaven,
the crack of cheap
corks that spoil
wine, the double chin
that fills out
the face and
falsifies the curves
hidden under chins, but
like newspaper on corners
between streets
in the hands of those

who have not read
in multitudes of skies,
but who speak hordes
on pavements covered in
plastic, blue plastic, orange
and green, different views
the same voices,
the same nightmares

PLASTIC

(n) synthetic or natural organic
materials shaped when soft and then
hardened, plastic children, plastic
adults, hardened adolescents,
cellulose derivatives and proteins,
carbon as in human (humane parents)
molded children, plastic children,
*molded plastic fags kiss girls (you're okay
in my eyes, son),* the entire meal was
served on plastic; (adj.) lie of a
lifetime, crackable, able to be spilled
on carpets, artificial, insincere, phony,
fake, *the plastic lives of fags,* pliable,
impressionable, *the plastic mind of a
youth,* of many youths, all youths,
sticks and stones, pummeled words
like electricity, like an injection of fire,
like a gun to the head in my own
hands, my life in my own hands

*One of the primary goals of the homosexual rights movement is
to abolish all age of consent laws and to eventually recognize
pedophiles as the 'prophets' of a new social order.*[46]

                    who do we
believe,
the walls
of business, the
steeples
of governors
the glass
paintings of
reverends
the bottles
the glass words
written
in blue
in black and red
on white?
I again
clasp
my hands
tightly
marble around
my neck;
though my hands
are only of skin
of bone
and sinew,
there is some
separation there,
not glass nor
spider, nor
shark of meat
but, perhaps
hands
that catch

my own thunder
my rain

> *The homosexual conduct of a parent—conduct involving a sexual relationship between two persons of the same gender—creates a strong presumption of unfitness that alone is sufficient justification for denying that parent custody of his or her own children or prohibiting the adoption of the children of others.... Homosexual conduct is, and has been, considered abhorrent, immoral, detestable, a crime against nature, and a violation of the laws of nature and of nature's God upon which this Nation and our laws are predicated. Such conduct violates both the criminal and civil laws of this State and is destructive to a basic building block of society—the family... It is an inherent evil against which children must be protected.*[47]

        why so
cryptic, you and they ask—
why these words, opaque?
It's engrained like
fear, like English
since birth, like bullies
like sticks—
faggot in the locker room
and stones—
homo in the hallway
        and death threats
I can hide
and choose to—
often   encrypted

These people are intellectually dishonest in just about everything they do or say. They start by pretending that it is just another form of love. It's sickening.[48]

GLASS

(n.) a hard, brittle, noncrystalline, transparent substance produced by fusion, the ordinary variety used for windows and bottles; a tall handless drinking container usually holding ice, a cold stone, obsidian, black coal, stone stick, held to the lips like poison, like a silent finger; a device to compensate for defective vision or to protect the eyes from dust or light, to protect from slime, from gore and the like, blood or knifed torso; careful study of the same, a mirror, reflection of the soul, *the glass called from his grave,* having been bottled in dirt, earth and mud of the soul; (v.) to reflect, *the trees glassed themselves onto the lake,* be careful! I am made of glass; the bottle is in fragments, shards

Hitler and his supporters were Satanists and homosexuals. That's just a true statement. The notion that is involved in homosexuality, the unbridled sort of satisfaction of human

> *passions leads to 'totalitarianism,' 'Nazism,' and 'communism.'*[49]

          I am a saint
said I,
said half man
not human
or an elephant, no
denim shirts
corduroy sugar—
in thunder, there is
sugar—
I am a saint
like John, like
salt

> *One might have that lifestyle, but if one promotes it as acceptable behavior... I don't think they should be a representative of this country.*[50]

SAINT

(n.) any of certain persons of exceptional holiness of life, formally recognized as such by the Christian Church: Saint Sebastian (homoeroticism); Saint Paul, the Apostle (lover of Saint Timothy); Saint Augustine, bishop of Hippo (turmoil over lover's death); Saint George of Cappadocia (bridegroom, lover of Christ); Saint Daniel (sexual minority, a homosexual, now a eunuch); Saint Bernard (breed of large canine, dog) *perhaps I am not a saint,* perhaps a murderer can be a saint, is a saint, esp. by canonization, glorification, the media and poetry, a fag, murderer of fags; a founder or sponsor of a movement against gay unions, against gay sex, against gay kissing and hugging, against passive loving, against liberation of the male or the elimination of hatred, a patron, a murderer, a holy person, consecration of, Kansas religion, picketers of, Wyoming burials, fags in earth, in dirt, who is the saint? I am not a saint.

♣♣♣♣♣

All the fag caterwauling, candlelight vigils, court orders, etc., can't buy Matt [Shepard] one drop of water to cool his tongue.[51]

       and now
I am cloudy
as they've dissipated
just disappeared like
rocky mountain
gold, like chocolate
and cookies,
crumbs left only
in the sky
on the horizon, between
eyes and sun
challenged again
by the peaks, the white
peaks, white again

You must love the Lord your God with all your heart, all your soul, and all your mind.' This is the first and greatest commandment. A second is equally important: 'Love your neighbor as yourself.' The entire law and all the demands of the prophets are based on these two commandments.[52]

    citrus slivers
on bitter tongue
squirt of thunder
in eyes, not salt,
sting of knuckles instead—
smudge of dirtied hands

again on ribcage, then
> the white
> light, the bright
> white light, colorless
> like heaven

illusioned, fooled
by drug addiction
in fists, fueled by
green, the alter
green, horned yet splashed
with white, simple white
not bright, not
colorless, not like—
soiled with sweat, painted
with the quince fruit
jacketed by wrinkled
age and hands of manicured
wooden benches,
plastic armor,
bacteria, troopers of
trust funds and prison—
holler at me from between
the bars, from behind
the steel closet door
> [the closet bottled
> and steel turned stone]

ARMOR

(n.) any covering worn as a defense against weapons; mechanized units of military forces, any protective covering, as on animals, insects or plants, armored insects, veiled (hidden), military troops (no longer silenced, yet still strong), the government listening, not to careless lies, the pews, the gays who will never come out, I say *I am only human,* as you, as evil, acceptable evil in humanity; anything that serves as protection, shallow eyes, leather shoes, uncombed hair with blond highlights, fuchsia plum; the pieces making up the parts of a metal external covering: *helmet,* covers the brain, thought; *visor,* the eyes, the imagination, truth; *ventail,* the smile, the quiver of lips, this poem; *beaver,* hides all glands in the neck, the jugular; *gorget,* halts any voice, any possible speech; *pauldrom,* encourages shrugs of the shoulders, stupidity or ambivalence; *rerebrace,* bicep covering, hiding any strength or courage; *couter,* flexible elbow guard, bendable, able to be swayed or encouraged; *vembrace*, conceals the pulse, the life-force, the area most often used in suicide; *gauntlet*, restricts the making of fists, binds; *breastplate*, the heart, hides emotion, conceals the soul; *lance rest*, support for a large weapon, a stick or a stone; *fauld*, flexible hips restricted by this armor; *cuisse*, coverage used to sharpen stance, to firm the leg position, to stand up straight; *poleyn*, flexible knee holder, made of stretchable silver, made to allow bowing but not used for this purpose; *greave*, grounding armor encasing the shins; *sabaton*, casket for the feet, six feet in stone, sealed upon earth, upon mud

As with smoking, homosexual behavior's 'second hand' effects threaten public health....Thus, individuals who choose to engage in homosexual behavior threaten not only their own lives, but the lives of the general population.[53]

        this building
will try,
though it has not fooled
but a billion
too many souls, unaccepted
and transferred

into nests guarded
by locked windows
noisy windows, cherished
in relationships
with the white tie,
yet again, white
and a chuckle
behind the gate
40 miles to destiny

> *When Will Perkins, chairman of Colorado for Family Values, was asked whether he supported [Paul] Cameron's call for quarantine of AIDS victims, he replied, 'It's a very complex question, but it has puzzled me that AIDS has not been handled the same way as any other deadly disease in an epidemic form.' Kevin Tebedo, a co-founder of Colorado for Family Values, has not been so shy, having been quoted as favoring tattooing and quarantine of those who test HIV positive.*[34]

                    it was him, not me
it was not
me, the best kid
I could be—
the saint, the bottle
hidden somewhere
a place I cannot
remember and I
could not tell, with
my hands, my steak
aching, my eyes
my teeth, they
are one and fixed

to up and down
but I tried, I tried
to hide the white

GATE

(n.) moveable barrier created of metal hands, able to be opened and closed; an opening permitting passage through an enclosure, to sneak out of the closet, to remove the armor; a path of great light, sincerity; the adornment of such an opening, *the gates of a walled city, the palace gate, the gates of heaven, the closed gate,* go away to religion, to the white house, *the heavenly gates are rusted by the tears of Jesus; Skiing,* an obstacle; the total of paid admissions; human cells, the temporary channel through which substances diffuse in or out of a cell; *Om.* an opening (a channel) to allow acceptance, hope, a breaking of the bottle, shattering, shards on the sand in the tide pool, high tide will relax into low and the breakage will be smoothed by waves; a dismissal, rejection, *my beliefs were given the gate; my gated dreams*

♣♣♣♣♣

You can say I'm a hater. But I would argue I'm a lover. I'm a lover of traditional families and of the right of children to have a mother and father. I would argue that the future of America hangs in the balance, because the future of the family hangs in the balance. Isn't that the ultimate homeland security, standing up and defending marriage?[35]

                    a movement
lighter
than my hands,
the president
of my body,
my energy dissipated
my apartment
in suits, black tie
homicide, walking alive
that rhymes
the routine rhyme
and makes cameras
smile, invoking an end
a satirical end
unbalanced and childlike
buy it from me, from
boiler room steam
immediate impulses
(too much killing)
undeleted, seemingly
unacceptable, a slasher;
O Jesus, these people,
when should I
expect this end?

That's what we're talking about. Whenever you're talking about gay rights, you're talking about giving somebody a gun to put at the head of anybody who disagrees with them, whether it's the Boy Scouts, whether it's a local dry-cleaning establishment or a giant corporation like Shell Oil.[56]

IMPULSE

(n.) the influence of a particular feeling or mental state, *I think under a violent impulse,* a sudden (involuntary) inclination prompting to action (the death of another teen, and another, then another *suicide*); a psychic drive or instinctual urge, a desire to be veiled, hidden in earth, to be dead and return again as a heterosexual human or an animal of any sexual preference in a kingdom where no stones are thrown, no sticks are broken and the bottles do not hold water or carbon; an impelling action or force driving onward or inducing motion, *my impulse is to corrupt the government and overthrow religion,* (I am a fag) a change in flow, current, a change in momentum

A form of national 'brainwashing' has been employed by the propagandists of the homosexual movement.[57]

a step down
to the left to

imagine the west
blue ocean, still brown
natural and considered,
chosen to be,
labeled, unchallenged,
ugly, uncircumcised
(retained—it continues)
the English language
is only fiction
"let's twist again"
yet realistically dark
like the neighbors, always
the neighbors, *see them
in the dictionary*, in the
middle, the solid
ground, the bottle
is still in the sand, hidden
deeply, sifted to a simple
picture, symbolism
hanging—
on walls, in the eyes
of its residents,
in the smudge
on the glass,
in the roots
of my scalp, my brown
hair, not brown, my
follicles dyed white,
as a saint or two kings
undress, my saints
my blue saints, not white

> *Eighty percent of the people that come to Transformation Ministries in Washington D.C. have been sexually molested and/or raped as children. We see that. We take an informal poll every six months, and the data is accurate. It keeps coming up constant, somewhere between 70 to 80 percent. We see high levels of divorce, high levels of alcoholism, very, very dysfunctional family situations.*[58]

    still the red,
the spilled red
on sidewalks or washed
mud, *in bedrooms,* not in
canes or nightsticks, nor
handcuffs
or tightropes, but
in fingers, in sturdy
clasps guarded by rings
and pencils, held
with steel suspenders
seasoned in fires
contained (retained,
controlled, repressed,
suppressed, stifled)
    held in check
captured, caged—
closeted

GROUND

(n.) the solid surface of the earth, soil, *stony ground;* a foundation or basis on which a belief or action rests, reason or cause (grounds for dismissal) you're a fag; a rationale for supporting one's position or opinion, but still, you're a fag or a woman, too much like a woman in a man's machine, faggot, a subject for discussion, for disapproval, for teachers of K though 12 to use sticks and stones and sway the minds of children, dead children now, in the ground, veiling the truth, exposing the wrists, the vambrace ineffective or invalid, ground level, but holding one's stance as one holds his ground in the palms, the dirt, dust and mud of earth, watered by ineffective (confused) teachers *go home to your wives and closet and pews (and let the fags teach)*

It's one thing to say, 'We have rights to jobs...we have rights to be left alone in our little corner of the world to do our thing.' It's

an entirely different thing to say, well, 'We're not only going to go into the schools, we're going to take your children and your grandchildren and turn them into homosexuals.' Now that's wrong.[59]

        I cannot
hear the birds
cannot see the smoke
in the east
it has somehow gone
from my fingers, evaporated
soluble clouds, estate
sales, water
in popcorn, candle
on nightstand, a reading light
the darkness
at dawn, somehow gone
a way of evolution—
may it ever leave me?
    let it
    avoid me, let it lift
    me with itself, into
    the skies, into the
    peppered sky
    the fences, stakes and
    boxes of protest, of
    revolution
    of militarized canons
        erupted
into apricots and curry
where they may eat
of silence, enjoy
their twos, their census

shall it plane off, or out
or into meetings,
disruptions, the long
weekends, flat bread, seven-second
spices, cracked and
flavored with olive oil
and the black and white
the grayscale dropping,
confident of jobs, though
penniless for the rice,
for cooks and cleaners
at home, for sitters
and teachers, do they know
I am all of these, I am
more than these? (I am thunder—
               and hope)

> *If the world accepts homosexuality as its norm and if it moves the entire world in that regard, the whole world is then going to be sitting like Sodom and Gomorrah before a Holy God. And when the wrath of God comes on this earth, we will all be guilty and we will all suffer for it.*[60]

    fags, the end
of the world
is on us, not
on the procreation of
too many to build
churches, *you're grounded*
    my gay son...

SPICE

(n.) pungent or aromatic substances of the anus derived from vegetable origin (usu. of orange vegetables) *I sniffed the spice of his anus,* used as seasonings, preservatives, etc. something that gives zest, enjoyment, gusto (a fag argues with a minister of family values) humor; a piquant, interesting element or quality, *his religious beliefs added spice to his argument* (also used as v.) *his religious brainwashing spiced up his lies; Archaic.* a small quantity of something, a trace, a bit, *a spice of hope*

> *[Homosexuality] is the opposite of love for God. It is a rebellion against God and God's natural order, and embodies a deep-seated hatred against true religion.*[61]

        listen to me
I love Jesus
I love God
I love You
    and Me
        have I not

used enough white
or blue? If they die—
    hanged, shot
the bullies
did not do it
    the privileged—
what's that I heard?
all of them, the tribes
of drumbeat
and dance?
down it trickles
to battle
fathers and sons
cigars on nipples
holy nipples, holy
children, cousins, uncles

UNCLE

(n.) brother of one's father or mother, an aunt's husband, a familiar term of address for an elderly man, trusted elder of a church congregation; *Slang.* a pawn-broker; *Informal.* Uncle Sam, the government (one who encourages others to fight a war, a battle, for a specific cause); to concede defeat, *to say uncle*; to give in

> *If you're involved in the gay and lesbian lifestyle, it's bondage. It is personal bondage, personal despair and personal enslavement.*[62]

        though it
does not belong
in courts or airplanes
like dogs, like snakes, like
elephants, what is it
but fundraising
for the castles, the walls
crumble
the closet walls
we must protect the walls
(in quotes) the boundaries

the donations, the rich
not Me
not My breath
upon the stones
    [I was in the river
    all over the river
    that's what they
    said, the impact
    through it all
    the uneasiness, the
    weary shells
    the pearl in the lips
    the toads like
    oxygen
    and I did not
    smile back
    at the angels; though
    I was able to laugh
    with them,
or was it cry—
    I did not sit
    or lie or move
    a false hand]
I did not displace
the handles
on her hips
the halos on their
glowing crops, I did not
merge
with the white
I kept clear, jogged
through the center
of the stage, in the clear

glass, washed underneath
the shore
  and here I am
  again, to stay
  for now—
it is not religion
  or God
  that spikes
  the stones, nor
  caps bottles—
  there is no
  disdain there
it is of your own disdain
  uninformed
    misled

SHORE

(n.) the land along the edge of an ocean, sea, river, etc.; a country, *my native shore,* a sexual preference, land (as opposed to sea or water); a supporting post or beam, esp. along the side of a building or dock or a ship; to support gov't subsidies, *to shore up falling corn prices,* (to shore religious movements, as in outlawing gay unions or ministers, *prop 8*); *Scot. and North Eng.* (v.) to threaten (someone), *religious law will shore any fag movement*

> *If marriage is radically redefined as a way of just affirming loving feelings of attraction, then equality will require allowing people who love dogs to marry dogs. And people who love ice cream to marry ice cream.*[63]

               it's Sunday
the one day
called rest, called
Sabbath, called boredom
and fear and
ambivalence for what's ahead—

prayer, Monday
a phenomenon, option
the biggest loser is
loss of the thumb
and now I am hungry
shook up
and out, at a bland
middle age, digging through
arid water, still
with an orange breeze
sour breath and
two more lines like
balloons flowing
into lungs and
doors closing
on careers, on grandma's hands
(I still do not trust her)
where does this come from—
what whispers of hers
lend color to the cherry trees
and vines planted
on church cement
in fertilized lawns? Why
doesn't anyone hear
these sounds? I'm calling
as loudly as I can, as loudly
as I know how—
    who corked the bottle
    again, with cement and
    concrete, with stone?

You have a teacher talking about his gayness. (The elementary school student) goes home then and says "Mom! What's gayness? We had a teacher talking about this today." The mother says "Well, that's when a man likes other men, and they don't like girls." The boy's eight. He's thinking, "Hmm. I don't like girls. I like boys. Maybe I'm gay." And you think, "Oh, that's, that's way out there. The kid isn't gonna think that." Are you kidding? That happens all the time. You don't think that this is intentional, the message that's being given to these kids? That's child abuse.[64]

CEMENT

(n.) any of various calcined mixtures
of clay and limestone, usually mixed
with water and sand and gravel to
form concrete used as building
materials; any soft, sticky substance
that dries hard and stone-like, like
sperm or spit from pulpits or restless
corneas, grit on hands, harmed by
endless turning of pages, esp. used
for mending broken objects or what is
considered broken, sex of two men;
anything that binds or unites, *time
cements friendship*; to unite, to cement
a relationship or deal, to join together
to make a better place, world (earth)
human, to become humane

*The Jews of Temple Beth Sholom are sinful, greedy, Hell-bound,
money-grubbing sodomites; and they have dedicated their
synagogue to be a gay and lesbian propaganda mill and
recruiting depot, soliciting young people to sodomy.*[65]

         the degrees
have risen
have warmed

though it is spring
with snow
on the ground
white snow, again
and again, the cold
the white
the snow

>Don't criticize and then you won't be criticized for others will treat you as you treat them.⁶⁶

SNOW

(n.) precipitation in the form of ice crystals, often intricately beautiful, formed directly from freezing water vapor in the air, white, soft; *Literary.* white blossoms, the white color of snow, still; cocaine, heroin; white spots or bands on a television screen caused by a weak signal (to hide behind this snow); to persuade or deceive, *I was snowed into believing everything,* I believed the white, the crystal white shards of broken bottles, yet the white of snow continues to be stoned (listen to Him) and sticked (v.)

God hates fags.[67]

           there's a large
gap there
between the zone
of slowing trains and
speeding cruise ships
of white and white
of snow and Jesus
a large gap

with lengthy lines
dark marker-like lines
on white
muscle-like lines, pink-
skinned [solo]
I look to the ground again
    alone, yet
    not alone

    Try to show as much compassion as your Father does.
    Never criticize or condemn, or it will come back on you.[68]

    he says
it is not white
and I believe him; it is
a thick, dark gap, black
the suit of a reverend
and he is not alone

SOLO

(adj.) a musical composition meant for performance by one person, alone, without a companion or partner; a group taking on a cause without the support of the government, neighbors, religious organizations, or even their parents; a flight in which the aircraft pilot is unaccompanied, an activity performed alone, without assistance, *solo flight, solo swim, solo speech, belief, or cause*; to scream alone, to be without help, without democracy, with one's own thoughts, distant, hidden under earth or inside a bottle

You will be dragged before the courts, and beaten in the synagogues, and accused before governors and kings of being my followers. This is your opportunity to tell them the good news.[69]

                    the charcoal
is black
but it illuminates
teaches duality,

how could I
know life if
I do not know
pain, death,
the stones and sticks
the bottle as veil
corked and rounded in
oceans of endless
graveled roads,
and how will I
know freedom
if I have not yet learned
how to hide?

the ending

These spices I've chosen, these
hives, these itches and
flaws, these
detestable things:

>that we too feel
>that we too scratch
>and bleed, that we too
>love God, even when
>we are only seen
>through the bottle

>it's tight in here
>and I can smell the garlic
>though I struggle to breathe—

>Emphasize the we:

>and now you know how we feel—
>sticked, stoned,
>bottled
>these messages
>bombarded
>yet still we survive
>out

DEFINITIONS DERIVED FROM:

Webster's New Universal Unabridged Dictionary. 1996 ed.

NOTES on QUOTES:

[1] Jesus Christ. *The Holy Bible, New Living Translation.* Copyright 1996, 2004 by Tyndale Charitable Trust.
[2] Pat Roberston. http://www.imdb.com/name/nm0731979/bio.
[3] Leonard P. Matlovich (July 6, 1943 – June 22, 1988). Inscribed on his tombstone.
[4] Gary Bauer, during the time of his presidency of the Family Research Council.
[5] Family Research Council press release, October 16, 1998, regarding the funeral of Matthew Shepard, the day of his funeral.
[6] Robert Knight.
[7] Anthony Falzarano, PFOX (Parents and Friends of Ex-Gays). Janet Parshall's *America*, February 27, 1996.
[8] Paul Volle, Chairman, Christian Coalition of Maine. *The Gay Agenda*, October 1998.
[9] Rick Santorum, in an interview with the Associated Press, April 22, 2003.
[10] Reverend Fred Phelps.
[11] Reggie White to the Wisconsin Assembly, March 25, 1998.
[12] Jesus Christ. *King James Bible* (Cambridge Ed.).
[13] Steven L. Anderson. Faithful Word Baptist Church, Tempe, AZ. From http://www.rightwingwatch.org/content/god-commands-you-kill-gays.

14 People for the American Way *Hostile Comate*, 1997, p. 15.
15 Banner developed by Americans For Truth About Homosexuality for a rally in support of Chick-fil-A.
16 Kristi Hamrick. From *Queer Families, Queer Politics: Challenging Culture and the State* by Mary Bernstein, Renate Reimann. Columbia University Press, 2001, p. 379.
17 People for the American Way *Hostile Climate*, 1998, p. 9.
18 Jesus Christ. *The Holy Bible, New Living Translation*. Copyright 1996, 2004 by Tyndale Charitable Trust.
19 Senator Michele Bachmann, referring to the gay community and same-sex marriage on the radio program *Prophetic Views Behind The News*, hosted by Jan Markell, March 20, 2004.
20 Rick Santorum, comparing homosexuality to being black. http://www.addictinginfo.org/2012/01/05/31-rick-santorum-quotes-that-prove-he-would-be-a-destructive-president/.
21 Anthony Falzarano.
22 People for the American Way *Hostile Climate*, 1998, p. 9.
23 Judith Reisman in a presentation at a conference for the Christian right in Colorado Springs, 1994.
24 Steven A. Schwalm, Family Research Council. *The Assault on Christians by the Militant Homosexual Movement*. http://www.frc.org/podium/pd98j2hs.html.
25 Michael Johnston. Family Research Council Web site, October 16, 1996.
26 Paul Cameron, as quoted by Mark E. Pietrzyk, in *News-Telegraph*, March 10, 1995.
27 Paul Cameron, speaking at the 1985 Conservative Political Action Conference. Rejected by the scientific community for fraudulent research and misrepresenting the research of others, Cameron was dropped from

membership in the American Psychological Association in 1984 for ethical violations concerning his biased research.

[28] Don Wildman, in a mailer from the American Family Association.

[29] Don Wildmon, American Family Association website, 2011.

[30] Richard G. Howe. *Homosexual in America – Exposing the Myths.*

[31] Westboro Baptist Church press release

[32] Gary Glenn, president of Michigan chapter of American Family Association, 2001.

[33] Reggie White. *Republicans Come Up Short Courting Black Conservatives,* by Terry M. Neal, washingtonpost.com staff writer, Monday, January 10, 2005; 6:00 AM.

[34] Dr. Laura Schlessinger radio show, June 10, 1999.

[35] Bryan Fischer, American Family Association Director of Issue Analysis for Government and Public Policy, 2010.

[36] Dr. Frank Simon, American Family Association of Kentucky. http://www.pfaw.org/press-releases/1998/08/religious-rights-hate-tactics-documented-hostile-climate-1998-edition.

[37] Paul Volle, Chairman, Christian Coalition of Maine. *The Gay Agenda.* October 1998.

[38] Alveda King, at a 1997 rally in Sacramento, California protesting proposed state legislation to extend anti-discrimination laws relating to housing and employment to gays and lesbians.

[39] Reverend Fred Phelps, Westboro Baptist Church.

[40] Paul Cameron quoted at http://www.biblebelievers.com/Cameron2.html.

[41] David Trosch. Former American Catholic priest.

[42] Pat Robertson. June 1998 while campaigning for president.
[43] Jesus Christ. *The Holy Bible, New Living Translation.* Copyright 1996, 2004 by Tyndale Charitable Trust.
[44] Pat Robertson.
[45] American Family Association press release, February 2010.
[46] Family Research Council.
[47] Chief Justice Roy Moore, 2002, in a statement from the Alabama State Supreme Court when ruling against a lesbian mother who was attempting to gain custody of her three children who had been in the custody of their father, her former husband.
[48] Former Senator Jesse Helms in an interview with *Variety* posted June 29, 1998. http://www.variety.com/article/VR1117478046?refCatId=1201.
[49] Alan Keyes. People For the American Way Foundation, *Hostile Climate*. 1997, p.26.
[50] Sen. Don Nickles in an interview on *Fox News Sunday*, June 21, 1998.
[51] www.godhatesfags.com.
[52] Jesus Christ. *The Holy Bible, New Living Translation.* Copyright 1996, 2004 by Tyndale Charitable Trust.
[53] Gary Glenn, president of Michigan chapter of American Family Association, 2001.
[54] Reported by Mark E. Pietrzyk of the *News-Telegraph*.
[55] Rick Santorum, July 2004. http://www.theatlanticwire.com/politics/2012/04/thank-you-rick-santorum-women/50976/.

[56] Robert Knight, Family Research Council. http://modernsocialworker.blogspot.com/2012/06/united-states-of-fear.html.
[57] Charles W. Socarides, M.D. *Thought Reform And The Psychology of Homosexual Advocacy*. Source: *Collected Papers from the NARTH Annual Conference, Saturday, 29 July 1995*.
[58] Anthony Falzarano.
[59] Pat Robertson, *The 700 Club*, September 17, 1992.
[60] Pat Robertson, *The 700 Club*, September 6, 1995.
[61] Steven A. Schwalm, Family Research Council. *The Assault on Christians by the Militant Homosexual Movement*. http://www.frc.org/podium/pd98j2hs.html.
[62] Senator Michele Bachmann, speaking at EdWatch National Education Conference, November 6, 2004.
[63] Daniel Heimbach, senior professor of Christian ethics at Southeastern Baptist Theological Seminary. http://www.verbicidemagazine.com/2012/06/19/top-ridiculous-anti-same-sex-gay-marriage-quotes/.
[64] Senator Michele Bachmann, speaking at EdWatch National Education Conference, November 6, 2004.
[65] Reverend Fred Phelps. *godhatesfags.com*.
[66] Jesus Christ. *The Holy Bible, New Living Translation*. Copyright 1996, 2004 by Tyndale Charitable Trust.
[67] The slogan and web url for the Westboro Baptist Church.
[68] Jesus Christ. *The Holy Bible, New Living Translation*. Copyright 1996, 2004 by Tyndale Charitable Trust.
[69] Jesus Christ. *The Holy Bible, New Living Translation*. Copyright 1996, 2004 by Tyndale Charitable Trust.

www.ingramcontent.com/pod-product-compliance
Lightning Source LLC
LaVergne TN
LVHW020935090426
835512LV00020B/3371